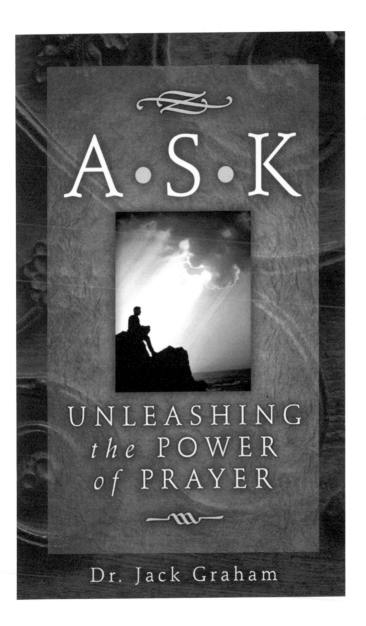

A·S·K

UNLEASHING *the* POWER *of* PRAYER

Dr. Jack Graham

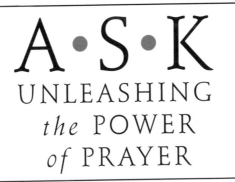

A · S · K

UNLEASHING
the POWER
of PRAYER

Dr. Jack Graham

P.O. Box 262627
Plano, TX 75026
1-800-414-7693 (1-800-414-POWER)
jgraham@powerpoint.org
jackgraham.org

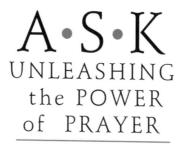

A·S·K
UNLEASHING
the POWER
of PRAYER

For information:
PowerPoint® Ministries
P.O. Box 262627
Plano, TX 75026
1-800-414-7693 (1-800-414-POWER)
jackgraham.org

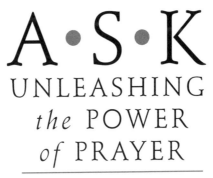

A·S·K
UNLEASHING
the POWER
of PRAYER

Dr. Jack Graham

CONTENTS

INTRODUCTION

Our world is in turmoil…unstable…full of pressures and uncertainties. And sometimes the problems can seem so overwhelming we wonder if there are any answers to the needs, to the troubles, to the tribulations we face.

But there is an answer. And that answer is found in prayer. In fact, God is looking for people like you and me who will so connect with Him in prayer that He can unleash His power through us. It is a power to overcome any trial, any difficulty, and any challenge. It's a power that can change our world!

When we learn to pray the kingdom way, there are amazing results. When we connect with God in prayer, we are given His very presence and power for living.

God promises us in Jeremiah 33:3:

> *Call to me and I will answer you, and will tell you great and hidden things that you have not known.*

So how do you learn to unleash the power of prayer? How can you know the power of God unleashed in your life? By going to the greatest authority on prayer, Jesus. Jesus lived a life of prayer. In fact, His life is a living prayer because we are told in the Bible:

HOW CAN YOU KNOW THE POWER OF GOD UNLEASHED IN YOUR LIFE? BY GOING TO THE GREATEST AUTHORITY ON PRAYER, JESUS.

> *Consequently, he is able to save to the uttermost those who draw near to God through him, since he always*

*lives to make intercession for them
(Hebrews 7:25).*

That's you and me! He continually,
consistently, fervently, and faithfully prays for
you and me.

Jesus, the very Son of God, is and was a
Man of prayer. In fact, there are ten prayers
given by Jesus that are recorded in
Scripture…prayers He prayed throughout His
life and ministry. He prayed at His baptism. He
prayed in the desert during times of temptation.
He prayed early in the morning. He prayed
before He chose His disciples. He prayed in the
Garden of Gethsemane. He prayed at the cross.

Jesus' life was a life of prayer. Is there
any wonder that His disciples, His most intimate
followers who observed this magnificent life
of prayer, asked, "Lord, teach us to pray"
(Luke 11:1)?

Now, it's impossible to understand
everything there is to know about prayer. It will
take an eternity for us to uncover and discover
the full impact and power of prayer in our lives.
But while we are here on this earth, we need to
learn to pray. We need to develop our prayer
lives so that we can unleash the power of prayer.

In Matthew 7:7-8, our Lord Jesus says:

> *"Ask, and it will be given you; seek, and
> you will find; knock, and it will be opened to
> you. For everyone who asks receives, and
> the one who seeks finds, and to the one who
> knocks it will be opened."*

Jesus invites you to this amazing adventure
of unleashing the power of prayer in your life. So
often the books we read and the messages we
hear regarding prayer put us on a deep guilt trip.
And rightfully so, because most of us struggle
with our personal prayer lives!

But beyond the guilt, we need to understand the great joy and privilege prayer really is. We need to grasp the exciting, enriching experience of prayer. We need to understand what God does

> WE NEED TO UNDERSTAND THE POWER THAT IS UNLEASHED IN PRAYER.

when His people pray. We need to understand the power that is unleashed in prayer.

Jesus offers an invitation to prayer to everyone...not simply to the super saints or the spiritually elite...but to every follower of Jesus. Every child of the Father is welcomed into His presence. He invites us to ask...to seek...and to knock.

CHAPTER ONE
ASK

In Matthew 6:5-8, Jesus instructs us on this journey of prayer:

"And when you pray, you must not be like the hypocrites. For they love to stand and pray in the synagogues and at the street corners, that they may be seen by others. Truly, I say to you, they have received their reward. But when you pray, go into your room [or your closet] and shut the door and pray to your Father who is in secret. And your Father who sees in secret will reward you. And when you pray, do not heap up empty phrases as the Gentiles do, for they think that they will be heard for their many words. Do not be like them, for your Father knows what you need before you ask him."

In this passage, Jesus begins by making two assumptions regarding prayer.

First, He assumes that we do pray. Three times in verses 5, 6, and 7 He says, "When you pray." Jesus assumes that as believers we pray. This identifies the simplicity and necessity of prayer. In fact, our very life is dependent upon it. It's like an infant who, in those first moments of life, takes a breath and receives life. Through prayer, we receive the breath and life of God!

It's been said that we can do more than pray *after* we pray, but we cannot do more than pray *until* we pray. No person comes to faith in Jesus Christ apart from believing prayer. We will never make a transforming impact upon the culture in which we live apart from prayer. There is no committed discipleship, there is no compelling witness, there is no effective parent, and there is no effective life without prayer. Jesus assumes that we know and understand the absolute necessity of prayer.

The second assumption Jesus makes is that we must learn more about prayer. Jesus assumes we need to be taught to pray. Why? Because we have problems with prayer! When it comes to prayer, we have problems with carelessness and prayerlessness.

THROUGH PRAYER, WE CAN NOT ONLY INTERCEDE FOR OTHERS, BUT WE CAN KNOW GOD INTIMATELY.

It can be pretty convicting when we think about our own prayer lives. We're so busy that we pray only sometimes. We pray now and then. But God desires so much more for us when it comes to prayer. Through prayer, we can not only intercede for others, but we can know God intimately. Through prayer, we can make a difference in this world...and yet we fail.

What is it about us that resists prayer? Even the apostle Paul recognized what a struggle prayer is when he noted in Romans 8:26, "We do not know what to pray for as we ought...." It's amazing to think that the great Christian Paul struggled in his prayer life! And so do we! Which is why we cry out with the disciples, "Lord, teach us to pray."

> WHICH IS WHY WE CRY OUT WITH THE DISCIPLES, "LORD, TEACH US TO PRAY."

Jesus welcomes our questions. He wants us to pray...to come to Him and ask Him for what is on our hearts. But how should we pray? There are two driving principles that teach us. And through those principles, we can begin to unleash the power of prayer.

"*B*UT WHEN YOU PRAY,

GO INTO YOUR ROOM [OR YOUR

CLOSET] AND SHUT THE DOOR

AND PRAY TO YOUR FATHER

WHO IS IN SECRET."

Don't Pray to Perform

Jesus begins His lesson on prayer by saying:

> *"When you pray, you must not be like the hypocrites."*

Now if Jesus tells us not to pray like hypocrites, it's pretty important that we understand what a hypocrite is. The word *hypocrite* comes from the Greek theater, and was used to denote someone who was an actor. And in Greek theater, actors would put on a mask to play various parts in a play.

WHEN WE PRAY AND PUT ON A PERFORMANCE... RATHER THAN *GENUINELY* PRAY... WE'RE SIMPLY PLAYING A PART.

What Jesus is saying is pretty clear. When we pray and put on a performance...rather than *genuinely* pray...we're simply playing a part.

When we hide our true identity—our self-righteousness—behind our own prayers and stand at center stage…we are just playing a part, we are acting. We are just pretending to pray. And that is hypocrisy.

Jesus said don't pray like the hypocrites because

> *"…they love to stand and pray in the synagogues and at the street corners, that they may be seen by others."*

There is nothing wrong with standing to pray. In fact, during those times, the Jewish people would often stand, lifting up holy hands in prayer to God. The posture is not the point here. Jesus is not condemning public prayer. The hypocrisy is that these men, who loved to stand and pray on the street corners and in the sanctuaries and the synagogues, did it to be seen by men.

That is the problem. There is the hypocrisy…to pray for the applause of men rather than the applause of God. Hypocrites are more interested in their own reputation than in personal righteousness. They desire the approval of men rather than the approval of God. So Jesus rips off the mask of phoniness and says that when you and I pray, don't pretend. Don't just pray with words that mean nothing. Don't pray to perform.

The only way I know how you and I can identify this in our lives is to ask ourselves, "Do I only pray when people are watching? Do I simply pray so others will think more of me or the best of me?" Those of us who are called upon to pray publicly must be very careful that we don't pray professional prayers. And the only way I know how to guard against this in my own life is to first engage the God of heaven through private and personal prayer. When I do that, then

I am ready for public prayer.

Jesus is really probing our motivation. So let me ask you, what's your prayer life like? Really, what's it like? Not just what men see, but what God sees. Is it truly your desire to draw near to God, to know Him, to talk with Him? So many Christians are all showcase and no warehouse. Everything's out front, but there's nothing on the inside. And that's what Jesus is

> SO LET ME ASK YOU, WHAT'S YOUR PRAYER LIFE LIKE? REALLY, WHAT'S IT LIKE?

warning us about here. Don't pretend to pray, but pray. And don't pray to perform.

But there's another kind of performance Jesus warns us about. It's found in verse 7 of this passage where He says:

> *"And when you pray, do not heap up empty phrases as the Gentiles do, for*

they think that they will be heard for their many words."

Jesus points to the ineffectiveness of the heathens' prayers…which are just a bunch of repetitious words. They just say the same thing over and over again. Saying prayers is not the same thing as praying prayers. Repetitious, routine, and rote praying is praying like the pagans, praying to perform before God. Today there are various kinds of prayers, including transcendental meditation, new age mysticism, and praying through beads. These kinds of rituals and routines represent the very things Jesus warned us about when we pray.

Don't just say the same things or repeat the same prayers again and again and again. Instead, pray from your heart!

And so Jesus gives us the first principle of unleashing the power of prayer. Don't

"AND WHEN YOU PRAY,

DO NOT HEAP UP EMPTY

PHRASES AS THE GENTILES DO,

FOR THEY THINK THAT THEY

WILL BE HEARD FOR THEIR

MANY WORDS."

pray to perform. A real disciple prays without performing.

PRAY WITH POWER

Instead of praying to perform, Jesus wants you and me to pray with power. The natural question is, "How do I pray with power?" The secret is found in private prayer. That's why Jesus tells us in verse 6 of this passage:

> *"But when you pray, go into your room [or your closet] and shut the door and pray to your Father who is in secret. And your Father who sees in secret will reward you."*

Notice the personal terms here.

> *"...When **YOU** pray, go into **YOUR** room...and **YOUR** Father who sees in secret will reward **YOU**."*

Every Christian, if they are to pray with

power, must find a place to pray privately. A place of solitude to pray secretly. Do you have a secret place? Do you have a quiet time when you say, "Lord, I want to know You, I want to see Your face"?

Now it's impossible, in my estimation, to really experience the presence of God in our lives apart from quiet, believing, secret prayer. You say, "Well, what about those verses that say we're to pray at all times and to pray everywhere?" That's certainly true! We are to pray continually, to pray constantly. We ought to always be just a breath away from prayer. But I've discovered in my own life that I won't pray everywhere and anywhere until I pray somewhere; until there is a place for private

> INSTEAD OF PRAYING TO PERFORM, JESUS WANTS YOU AND ME TO PRAY WITH POWER.

prayer. Jesus called it a closet.

He could have been referring to the treasure house, a little room where they kept the treasures of the house. It doesn't matter where the place is. You just need to find that place of solitude...for private prayer...if you are to pray with power.

YOU NEED TO FIND A PRIVATE PLACE TO PRAY BECAUSE THAT IS WHERE THE FATHER IS!

It reminds me of a woman named Susanna Wesley. Because she had so many children, she could never find time to be alone to pray. So she would just go to the kitchen and throw her apron over her head and pray. Good for her! Whatever it takes! Just find that place where you can be alone to pray.

Jesus would often get up very early in the morning and find a place of private prayer and engage the Father in conversation there. He would go to the mountainsides to pray. He would go to the lonely places to pray. He would pray in the desert. He would pray in the Garden of Gethsemane, which, in particular, seemed to be a special place of prayer for Jesus. He would always find a place He could pray privately.

Now, the reason we need a private place to pray is because "…your Father…is in secret…." Did you catch that in verse 6 above? You need to find a private place to pray because that is where the Father is!

The clutter of life, the demands of life, the pressures of your day and my day take us in directions that we can't even begin to anticipate as we begin each day. And the only way to be ready for those demands is to get in the secret place where the Father is.

The New International Version of the Bible translates Matthew 6:6 as "pray to your Father, who is unseen...." In other words, when we pray in the secret place, God is not far away...out there somewhere...but He is in the room, unseen, invisible, but present. In fact, God promises His presence when we pray like this.

But there are times we wonder about His presence, don't we? We wonder, "Lord, are You really there? Lord, do You really hear me? Lord, are my prayers getting above the ceiling?"

Well, they don't have to get above the ceiling if God is in the room! And the Father waits for us and welcomes us when we are in His presence in that secret place of prayer. You can be assured that God sees and God hears.

Prayer in the secret place is not self-talk or a psychological pump-up. It is actually conversing with God, communing with God, relating to God...and He to us. His very presence fills the smallest place and the most secret part of our lives.

Now, Jesus says an amazing thing in verse 6. He says that if you pray like this, He "will reward you."

Many Christians don't understand that the Christian life is a greatly rewarded life. In fact, you find that truth throughout the New Testament. But few people ever understand that when you pray the kingdom way…when you pray in secret and in all sincerity…you will be rewarded.

PRAYER IN THE SECRET PLACE IS NOT SELF-TALK OR A PSYCHOLOGICAL PUMP-UP. IT IS ACTUALLY CONVERSING WITH GOD, COMMUNING WITH GOD, RELATING TO GOD…AND HE TO US.

I believe the Bible tells us that there will be three rewards for those who pray. First, there will be a heavenly reward. God will reward in heaven those who pray here on earth.

Why? Because they are the ones who make the greatest impact upon time and eternity. Praying Christians change the destinies of men and the histories of nations. And when we get to heaven, many who have prayed in their closets—who never preached on platforms, who never taught in public assemblies, who were never identified as great public leaders—will be greatly rewarded.

WHEN YOU GO TO GOD IN THAT SECRET PLACE AND ASK HIM IN ALL SINCERITY, HE HEARS YOU, AND HE WILL ANSWER YOUR PRAYERS.

But not only is there the reward of heaven, there's a second reward. And that is the reward of answered prayer. Honest prayer is heard. Hypocritical prayer is not heard! God answers honest prayer.

Now that's a simple statement that even a child could make. But when you think about it, this is an incredibly profound thought. God answers prayer! In James 4:2-3, we are told:

> *You do not have, because you do not ask. You ask and do not receive, because you ask wrongly, to spend it on your passions.*

The reward of honest and genuine prayer is answered prayer. When you go to God in that secret place and ask Him in all sincerity, He hears you, and He will answer your prayers. You unleash the power of prayer when you pray that honest prayer in secret! But you have to ask!

Then there is one more reward for those who pray. And that reward is prayer itself. Prayer is its own reward. This is what I mean.

When you and I pray, we are empowered for living. We are better moms and dads, we are better business partners, we are better people. Prayer is the bottom line for believers if we are

OU DO NOT HAVE,

BECAUSE YOU DO NOT ASK.

YOU ASK AND DO NOT RECEIVE,

BECAUSE YOU ASK WRONGLY, TO

SPEND IT ON YOUR PASSIONS.

to live lives truly empowered by God's Spirit.

Pastor and author Peter Lord once said, "What we are on our knees alone with God is what we are. The rest is just religious talk."

Prayer is the bottom line for bona fide believers. It is who you are as a Christian. And when you pray in secret and in sincerity, your life will be transformed. Now, the world won't understand why you are so different. Why you have such joy. Why you have such peace. Why you have such a love for God and such a love for people. But you can't help but be transformed when you've been in prayer…when you've been in the very presence of God Himself.

> PRAYER IS THE BOTTOM LINE FOR BONA FIDE BELIEVERS. IT IS WHO YOU ARE AS A CHRISTIAN.

Because that is the reality of praying in

secret. It is in that place that God meets you…that you enter the holy of holies through Jesus Christ…and that your life becomes a sanctuary of praise to God.

So the basis for praying with power is through secret and sincere prayer. And there are two characteristics of this type of prayer.

The first is that you pray with confidence. If you want to pray with power, you must come to God like a little child talking to a caring father. And you can pray with confidence because He is your Abba Father…your dear Father.

For some believers today, it is really hard to see God as loving, caring, and available because they have grown up in homes where the father was absent. As a result, it's hard to see God as someone who is there for them and cares for them.

Absentee fathers are one of the biggest problems in America today. And this has huge ramifications for the future generation.

But that's not the only problem. While some fathers are absent, other fathers are apathetic and weak and fail to lead their families spiritually. Yet others are angry and take that anger out on the family. Still others are affectionless and never take the time to show their children the affection they need.

That's why there are some who read of God being Father and say, "If God's a Father like my father, I don't want anything to do with Him."

SO IF YOU ARE TO UNLEASH THE POWER OF PRAYER, YOU NEED TO COME TO GOD AS YOUR FATHER...WITH CONFIDENCE.

Well, God's not a Father like any human father. You can rest assured that this Father will never fail you. Even if your earthly father has failed you, you have a heavenly Father who will *never* fail you.

Now, some believe we need to jettison all references to God the Father because it's an outdated, outmoded term. Absolutely not! Our God is our Father...and our Father is the One who invites us into His presence...who desires for us to come to Him as a compassionate and loving Father. Which is why we can—with confidence—come boldly to the throne of grace (Hebrews 4:16).

So if you are to unleash the power of prayer, you need to come to God as your Father...with confidence. Even if you have experienced a father who is distant and detached, understand today that your heavenly Father is always loving...compassionate...and available.

By the way, as a man and a father, one of the most important things you can learn in life is to be a man of God. That includes being a man of prayer and loving your family...starting with your children's mother. If you want to love your children, start by loving their mother unconditionally. And model for your children the kind of God you want them to someday know...loving, compassionate, understanding, available.

So God loves us perfectly. And He invites us into His arms and welcomes us into His presence, which is why we can pray with confidence.

But not only are we to pray with confidence, we are to pray with reverence. Jesus, in the Lord's Prayer, began with the following phrase:

"Our Father in heaven, hallowed be Your name" (Matthew 6:9, NKJV).

Our Father is in heaven, He is holy, and His name is hallowed and exalted. And while we are to approach Him as little children, it must always be with love, respect, and devotion. Never flippantly or casually, but lovingly.

SO GOD LOVES US PERFECTLY. AND HE INVITES US INTO HIS ARMS AND WELCOMES US INTO HIS PRESENCE, WHICH IS WHY WE CAN PRAY WITH CONFIDENCE.

Now, some believe that "Abba Father" means "Daddy Father." Well, I'm okay with that, but it's not really what the Bible is saying. Abba Father doesn't translate to Daddy Father. *Abba* is the word that an immature child in the Middle East would use. In fact, if you go to the Middle East today, you can hear little children tagging along by the side of their fathers saying, "Abba, Abba, Abba, Abba."

And when the Bible refers to Abba Father,

it is encouraging us to approach God like an immature child who approaches his Father with intimacy.

I believe the best translation of Abba Father is not Daddy Father, but rather "Dear Father" or "Loving Father" or "Gracious Father." It is the Father who is hallowed…the One who is revered.

In Psalm 103:13, we are told:

> …*the LORD shows compassion to those who fear him.*

So we are not only to approach God in prayer with confidence, we are to approach Him with reverence and respect. There is a holy fear that should bring us into His presence. That fear and reverence should not drive us from His presence, but bring us into His presence, knowing He will have compassion on us when we fear Him.

...THE LORD

SHOWS COMPASSION TO THOSE

WHO FEAR HIM.

So we are to pray with confidence, pray with reverence, and then finally, we are to pray with obedience.

When Jesus says in Matthew 7:7 that we are to ask and seek and knock, have you ever discovered that this is an acrostic? **A**sking, **S**eeking, **K**nocking.

A - S - K

God wants us to keep on asking…to keep on seeking…to keep on knocking. That is what it means to pray with obedience. Not babbling like the pagans…with long speeches. Not with the pretension or the performance of an actor. Not thinking that somehow the length or style of your prayers is what will move the hand of God. But praying by asking, seeking, and knocking… with a heart that is crying out in faith to Him.

Some people pray with no intention of

getting right with God. They see God as some sort of genie who will respond if they pray a certain prayer…but their heart is not right. They think that somehow they can manipulate God to do what they want Him to do.

But if you pray asking, seeking, and knocking in obedience and submission to Him, you can count on God to answer your prayers. Do you need guidance? Do you need a job? Do you need a helpmate in life? Do you need health? Do you need healing? Do you need strength? Do you need grace? Whatever you need, child of God, you can bring it and A-S-K… and your Father will hear you. And what I have found over the years is that when you keep on asking, keep on seeking, and keep on knocking, the answer is already on the way!

There was a man by the name of Father Buckner who founded the Buckner Children's Home back at the turn of the century. Now,

Father Buckner was a godly man of prayer. On one occasion, money was tight, and they were in danger of going under because they couldn't pay the bills. And one of the bills they owed was something like $17.

So Father Buckner got down on his knees in the dining room of that little home, and he began to pray. He said, "Oh God, You promised Your provision. You promised to take care of these children. So Lord, I'm asking You to please provide for us what we need."

> BUT IF YOU PRAY ASKING, SEEKING, AND KNOCKING IN OBEDIENCE AND SUBMISSION TO HIM, YOU CAN COUNT ON GOD TO ANSWER YOUR PRAYERS.

Having prayed… asking, seeking, and knocking…he got up, and as he was thinking about his prayer, he looked out into the backyard of that orphanage. There he saw some big pecan trees. He sensed God prompting him, so he got the kids together and they went out and shook those trees for all they were worth. Pecans began falling all around them, and they ended up filling a big bushel basket full of pecans. They then took them down to the Farmer's Market in Dallas and sold them for exactly the price they needed to get out of debt.

GOD IS AT WORK WHEN WE PRAY IN OBEDIENCE TO HIM. WHEN WE ASK...SEEK... KNOCK IN THE QUIET AND SECRET PLACE, GOD WILL HEAR OUR PRAYERS.

When old Father Buckner told the story, he would often say, "When I think about it, even while I was down on my knees praying, 'God, when are You ever going to come through? God, when are You ever going to answer my prayer? God, please!' I now remember that pecans were hitting the roof."

You see, God is at work when we pray in obedience to Him. When we ask…seek…knock in the quiet and secret place, God will hear our prayers. And we will begin to unleash the power of prayer.

CHAPTER TWO
SEEK

Not only are we to ask, Jesus tells us in Matthew 7:7 we are to seek. Jesus tells us in that verse:

> *"Ask, and it will be given to you;*
> *seek, and you will find; knock, and it will be*
> *opened to you."*

Now, Jesus gave us this model for prayer so that we might learn to pray. In the last chapter, we discovered what it really means to A-S-K… and we learned the foundation for unleashing the power of prayer. But there is a second component you must understand if you are to unleash the power of prayer. That is to *seek*.

Most people don't understand what it really means to seek. To seek in prayer is to surrender your will to the will of God…to submit your way to the ways of God.

In Matthew 6:9-13, Jesus taught us how to pray in His master prayer, the model prayer, what is known as the Lord's Prayer. In verses 9 and 10 of that passage, Jesus says:

NOTICE THAT WHAT JESUS SOUGHT IN HIS PRAYER WAS GOD'S WILL…GOD'S WAY: "YOUR KINGDOM COME."

"In this manner, therefore, pray: Our Father in heaven, hallowed be Your name. Your kingdom come. Your will be done on earth as it is in heaven" (NKJV).

Notice that what Jesus sought in His prayer was God's will…God's way: "Your kingdom come. Your will be done on earth as it is in heaven."

Now, we know that God's will is not always

done on earth as it is heaven, otherwise we wouldn't be encouraged to pray for the will of God to be done on earth as it is in heaven! We live in a world suffering the consequences of sin, and God's will is not always perfectly done on earth even though He is sovereign over all the events and circumstances of our lives. Our world is filled with murder, hate, horrible accidents, terrorism, brokenness…all of which is not a part of the will of God. Which is why we are to pray that the will of God be done. Because in God's will is that which is perfect, true, pure, and all that is good.

To unleash the power of prayer, we must seek God's will in our prayers. What many Christians don't understand is that the power of prayer is not somehow twisting God's arm or manipulating God's mind…all of which is really a feeble attempt at trying to get our own way. Unleashing the power of prayer comes from adjusting our will to the will of God. It is asking Him to bend our will to His will.

It's been said that prayer is not *changing* God's mind but *finding* God's mind. I think that's a pretty good description of what it means to seek! Because in seeking God and seeking His will, we discover how to live.

In 1 John 5:14-15, we are told:

> *And this is the confidence that we have toward him, that if we ask anything according to his will he hears us. And if we know that he hears us in whatever we ask, we know that we have the requests that we have asked of him.*

We unleash the power of prayer when we pray for the will of God! It has been said that nothing lies outside the reach of prayer except that which lies outside of the will of God. So when we pray, seeking the will of God for our lives, we take another step in unleashing the power of prayer!

Now, when you seek God's will in prayer…when in your prayers you seek His will here on earth as it is done in heaven…you will learn what God wants to do with your life. Did you catch that?! *You will learn what God wants to do with your life.*

This is such an important and life-changing truth, I want to take the rest of this chapter to unfold it for you. I want to show you how you can pray, knowing that you are praying in the will of God…and in the process, discovering, discerning, developing, and doing the will of God in your life.

PRAY FOR THE WILL OF GOD

The first thing you need to do is to actually pray for the will of God. Now that's a simple enough idea, but I believe that many Christians have never discovered how to unleash the power of prayer because they have never sought to know and do God's will.

God's will is life's greatest privilege. In fact, God chooses for you what you would choose for yourself, if you had sense enough to choose it! And because you and I don't have sense enough...and because we don't have an understanding of the big picture of what is needed in our lives...we need to pray that God would do His will in our lives.

If you and I are to unleash the power of prayer, we must in fact pray for the will of God. It is something that we're to long for— something that we're to love, yearn for, and yield to. We are to pray earnestly and energetically for the will of God. We are to be like the psalmist who says in Psalm 40:8, "I desire to do your will, O my God...."

Do you desire or delight to do the will of God? If not, it's probably because you have a wrong impression of God's will. The will of God is not something that we *have* to do, it is something that we *get* to do.

The Lord Jesus is the best example of this. Jesus submitted His will to the will of the Father—even to the point of death. And what glory came from that! In Philippians 2:8-11, we are told:

> *And being found in human form, he*
> *humbled himself by becoming obedient to*
> *the point of death, even death on a cross.*
> *Therefore God has highly exalted him and*
> *bestowed on him the name that is above*
> *every name, so that at the name of Jesus*
> *every knee should bow, in heaven and on*
> *earth and under the earth, and every tongue*
> *confess that Jesus Christ is Lord, to the*

glory of God the Father.

Praying for the will of God is to pray for His glory in your life. And when you get His glory, you get your good. God wants what is best for each one of us. And the happiest, best place on earth is to be right in the center of God's will.

Jim Elliot, the martyred missionary, wrote in his diary, "God always gives the best to those who leave the choice with Him."

To do the will of God is the greatest achievement. And when we seek His will, He will reveal it to us. Remember, God *wants* you to know His will. He's not reluctant. Prayer is not overcoming God's reluctance to share His will with you, but rather, it is laying hold of His highest willingness to bless you.

I love the definition of success which says, "Success is the progressive realization of the will of God for our lives."

When you seek the will of God through prayer, He will provide you the progressive realization and actualization of His will for your life. By progressive, I mean God will reveal His will for you step by step, day by day. He will show the way to you if you will call upon Him…if you will truly seek Him and ask Him to show you.

> HE WILL SHOW THE WAY TO YOU IF YOU WILL CALL UPON HIM…IF YOU WILL TRULY SEEK HIM AND ASK HIM TO SHOW YOU.

As a pastor, people often ask me for counsel and advice on all kinds of issues, and I'm happy to help when I can. But often I simply ask folks, "Have you prayed about this? Have you asked God about this?" Because I can't imagine someone asking Jack Graham for advice before they ask God for advice. They often don't realize that He will show them the way if they will only ask!

I love Proverbs 4:18:

> *But the path of the righteous is like the light of dawn, which shines brighter and brighter until full day.*

I've reached a stage in life that I thought would never come. The stage when the dawning of the day…that first part of the day early in the morning…is what I enjoy as the best part of the day. Now, when I was younger I used to think, "Man, when I get a little older and I have a little more free time, I'm going to sleep in every day!" But now I've discovered the dawn of a new day…the beauty of the rising of the sun. There's nothing quite like the stillness and grandeur of the sun when it comes up. There's nothing quite like the sun when it begins to peek up over the horizon and turn the gray of the dawn to a beautiful red…and then burst forth with all its glory into a new day. And as the day moves on, of course, the sun rises higher and higher and

 UT THE PATH OF THE

RIGHTEOUS IS LIKE THE LIGHT

OF DAWN, WHICH SHINES

BRIGHTER AND BRIGHTER

UNTIL FULL DAY.

higher until the noon day when everything is bright and beautiful.

Well, that's what Proverbs 4:18 says about the will of God. That progressively...

SO WHEN YOU SEEK THE WILL OF GOD IN PRAYER, YOU WILL DISCOVER THE WILL OF GOD FOR YOUR LIFE.

...the path of the righteous is like the light of dawn, which shines brighter and brighter until full day.

If you want that kind of day in your life, you need to pray for the will of God. And as He reveals it to you, follow His pathway for your life. When you do, your life will get brighter and brighter. It's like the great old Gospel song:

I walk with the King, alleluia.
I walk with my King, praise His name.
No longer I roam, my soul faces home.

I walk and I talk with the King.

So when you seek the will of God in prayer, you will discover the will of God for your life. But you need to pray for the will of God. In fact, make it your prayer every day. Get up and face the day by saying, "Lord, Your will is what I seek. All I want is Your purpose, Your plan in my life. I want to be on Your agenda this day and in the days ahead."

Make a commitment to pray for the will of God. That is the very first step in seeking God's will and discovering God's will…and unleashing the power of prayer in your life.

PURSUE THE WILL OF GOD

While the first step of seeking God's will is to actually pray for the will of God, you must take that desire one step further. You must pursue it continually through prayer. It is not a one-time deal.

In the original language, the verb *asking* literally means to keep on asking. The verb *seeking* means to keep on seeking. And the verb *knocking* means to keep on knocking. Asking, seeking, and knocking are to be continuous efforts as we desire to know the will of God.

Now, you may be wondering what the difference is between asking, seeking, and knocking. This may help:

- Asking is petitioning prayer.
- Seeking is perceiving prayer (as you begin to discern and discover God's will).
- Knocking is persistent prayer.

And continually asking, seeking, and knocking is the sum total of pursuing the will of God. My prayer is that you will make it your purpose above all others.

If this is your desire, let me give you three

principles that will help you as you pursue the will of God in prayer.

1. *THE SURRENDER PRINCIPLE*

Read carefully the words of Romans 12:1-2:

I appeal to you therefore, brothers, by the mercies of God, to present your bodies as a living sacrifice, holy and acceptable to God, which is your spiritual worship. Do not be conformed to this world, but be transformed by the renewal of your mind, that by testing you may discern what is the will of God, what is good and acceptable and perfect.

That is the surrender principle. If you are serious about pursuing God's will in prayer, you ought to mark, memorize, and meditate on these two verses.

DO NOT BE CONFORMED

TO THIS WORLD, BUT BE

TRANSFORMED BY THE RENEWAL

OF YOUR MIND, THAT BY TESTING

YOU MAY DISCERN WHAT IS THE

WILL OF GOD, WHAT IS GOOD

AND ACCEPTABLE AND PERFECT.

To understand these two verses, you need to know that the 12th chapter of Romans is a response to the first 11 chapters of Romans. These 11 chapters describe the great grace of God…that while we were sinners, judged guilty by a holy God, Christ died to give us new life. There is no longer any condemnation for those who are in Christ Jesus. And that's when the apostle Paul writes, "I appeal to you therefore…."

Therefore, because God has been so gracious and merciful to you and me, He now begs us to offer ourselves as a living sacrifice to Him—in surrender to Him. As the great song of the faith says so perfectly:

Love so amazing, so divine
Demands my soul, my life and my all.

Surrender isn't a word we like very much because it speaks of capitulation or compromise. Surrender speaks of losing. And in a world that glorifies winners, we don't want anything to do with losing. Yet God says to the believer, "You are to surrender your life to Me."

Surrendering to God and His will carries the idea of complete consecration. And it's more than commitment. It means to take your hands off of your life and to put yourself completely on the altar. It means to yield yourself...to give yourself...completely to Him. That is surrender.

We throw around the word *commit* quite a bit today. We commit to Christ, we commit to the church, we commit to our marriages...all sorts of things. And commitment is a good word. But consecration means something even more.

Years ago, my friend Adrian Rogers was preaching in Romania, and the Romanian pastor was translating for him. In his sermon, Dr. Rogers used the word *commit*. And after the service was over, the pastor turned to Dr. Rogers and said, "You know, in our language, we really have no word that describes 'commit' for our faith. We don't really talk about 'commit' here." He then went on to say, "You Americans love to talk about commit because you like to be in control. In our country, we talk about surrender and consecration."

When you commit to something, you can "un-commit" what you commit...like so many do in marriage. But when you consecrate yourself...when you surrender...that is something entirely different. It means you've been captured by Christ, and, therefore, you are surrendered to Him. It's the decision that says, "Lord, Your kingdom come in my life. I get off the throne of my life. Lord, You take charge...You take command of my life."

Give yourself completely to God. Allow Him to be the Lord of your life—all of it! Jesus doesn't want 95% of your life. He wants…and He deserves, desires, and demands…*all* of your life.

Some people are too arrogant or prideful to surrender their lives to God. Others are afraid to surrender their lives to God. But when you surrender all to Him, you can trust Him. And let me assure you, God does have a wonderful plan for your life. When you give yourself unreservedly to Him, He will do His very best for you. You can give Him everything and anything. Jeremiah 29:11 says:

> *"For I know the plans I have for you, declares the LORD, plans for wholeness and not for evil, to give you a future and a hope."*

God is not a tyrant. He is our loving, holy, and heavenly Father. He is our dear Father who can be trusted with our families, with our future, with our fears. We can give Him…and trust Him with…everything.

You see, surrender is not limiting, it's *liberating*. In fact, the key to life is surrender.

And allow me to let you in on a little secret: If you don't surrender to Jesus, you'll surrender to something else. You'll surrender to chaos or confusion. You'll surrender to the opinions of others. Or you'll surrender to habits that you can't control. You will surrender to something or someone. The question is, will you surrender your life to the Lord Jesus Christ? Will you say, "Yes, Lord; whatever the question is, Lord, the answer is yes. Whatever you want me to do Lord, the answer is yes!" Because the minute you say, "No, Lord," He's no longer Lord of your life.

You can say "No" to God. You can say "Lord" to Him. But you can't say "No, Lord."

That's a contradiction. Do you understand that? If He is to be your Lord, the answer must always be, "Yes, Lord, I surrender; I give my life."

Mary, the mother of Jesus, is another good example of someone who was surrendered to God and His will. When she was told that she would give birth to the Savior of the world, she said, "How can these things be, I've never known a man?" She didn't understand it…she couldn't comprehend it. And yet she said,

> *"Behold, I am the servant of the Lord; let it be to me according to your word"* (Luke 1:38).

My prayer for you is that this will be your response to God today. That you will also say, "Lord, let it be to me according to Your Word."

While we don't always know the what, the when, the where, the why, or the how of God's will, we can trust God when we surrender our

"BEHOLD, I AM THE

SERVANT OF THE LORD; LET IT

BE TO ME ACCORDING TO

YOUR WORD."

lives to Him. And again, the supreme example of that is Jesus Himself who sweated blood in the Garden of Gethsemane, pouring out His life in prayer, surrendering His will to the will of the Father, declaring, "…not as I will, but as you will" (Matthew 26:39).

YOU SURRENDER TO GOD BY MAKING IT YOUR AIM, YOUR AMBITION, YOUR AGENDA TO PLEASE HIM.

A number of years ago, I discovered a short, succinct, powerful little verse in my study of the Scripture. I wrote it down on a card and put it in my wallet to carry as a reminder. It's 2 Corinthians 5:9, which says, "So whether we are at home or away, we make it our aim to please him."

You surrender to God by making it your aim, your ambition, your agenda to please Him. If that is indeed your aim, you will surrender your will to His will. So give your life as a living sacrifice to Him today.

Now, of course, the problem with a *living* sacrifice is that it can crawl on and off the altar. That's why we have to be willing to pray every day, "Lord, today I'm going to crawl on the altar and surrender all to You." Because it is in prayer that we surrender.

I know that when I'm not consistent in my prayer life, I start taking charge of things. But when I'm in the place of prayer, surrendering my will and my way to God, then I am able to give Him my family, my future, my ministry, my everything.

John Wesley wrote a prayer for his students that is still prayed today in the Methodist Church at the beginning of the year. It's a wonderful prayer and this is what it says:

"I'm no longer my own, but Yours. Put me to what You will. Rank me with whom You will. Put me to doing. Put me to suffering. Let me be employed for You or laid aside for You, exalted for You, or brought low for You. Let me be full. Let me be empty. Let me have all things. Let me have nothing. I freely and wholly yield all things to Your pleasure and Your disposal."

If you are wondering whether you are truly surrendered to God, let me ask you a few questions:

- Is there any place you would not go for God?
- Is there anything you would not do for Him?
- Is there anything you would not say for Him?
- Is there anything you would not give to Him?

- Is there anything you would not offer to Him?
- Can you say, "Lord, Your will, anywhere, anytime, at any cost"?

If you can, then that's surrender! You know you have applied the surrender principle. And if you can't say these things, then let me encourage you to surrender to Him today. Because your best day…the very best day you will ever live…is when you say "Yes" to the Lord Jesus Christ.

2. THE SCRIPTURE PRINCIPLE

In order to discern and discover the will of God, you not only have to surrender, you also have to saturate your mind with the Word of God. That's the Scripture principle. As Jesus says in John 15:7:

> *"If you abide in me, and my words*

"IF YOU ABIDE IN ME,

AND MY WORDS ABIDE IN YOU,

ASK WHATEVER YOU WISH, AND

IT WILL BE DONE FOR YOU."

abide in you, ask whatever you wish, and it will be done for you."

So it's not only surrendering to the will of God, but abiding in the Word of God.

You can never know what God wants you to do until you first know what God has said. And what God has said is in His Word. In fact, so much of the will of God is already revealed in the Bible, which is why we are to read, reflect on, and review the Word of God. We are to meditate on it, memorize it, and mark it. We are to study God's Word, and then we're to store up God's Word in order that we might know the will of God.

Now, I know it's impossible to study the Bible all day long. But I'll tell you what you can do. You can *think* about God's Word throughout your day. You can review it in your mind, you can remember His promises, and you can reflect upon it as you go about your day. It's easy to do a daily quiet time, go to Bible study, listen to Christian radio, view a study video, or go to church…but never really have the Word of God penetrate your heart and mind. What God wants us to do is to hide His Word in our hearts and then meditate on it…contemplate it…and consider it throughout our day.

David, who is described as a man after God's own heart, said, "Oh how I love your law! It is my meditation all the day." If we are to understand God's will, we need to saturate our hearts and minds with His Word.

As you do, God will bring to remembrance the word that you need. God will show you a way. God will give you a promise through an open door you would have never known. Because God shares His secrets with His friends. God has no favorites, but He does have friends.

And He shares His secrets with His friends.

So when you hear a message or you go to a Bible study or you read God's Word, take it in, think it through, pray it in, and live it out day after day. The Word of God and the will of God are inseparably linked together. God guides us through His Word. In prayer, we speak to God. In Bible study, God speaks to us. That's why it is impossible for you to know and to do the will of God unless you are willing to take time to think about the will of God through the Word of God.

Through His Word, God will show you His will. As Psalm 119:105 says:

> *Your word is a lamp to my feet and a light to my path.*

3. THE SPIRIT PRINCIPLE

As we seek the will of God through prayer,

we have looked at the surrender principle and the Scripture principle. The third principle is the Spirit principle.

> WE CAN BE LED SUPERNATURALLY, SUBJECTIVELY, INWARDLY, AND PERSONALLY BY THE SPIRIT OF GOD. GOD TAKES HIS WORD, AND, BY HIS SPIRIT, HE THEN LEADS US.

In Romans 8:14, the apostle Paul writes:

> *For all who are led by the Spirit of God are sons of God.*

We can be led supernaturally, subjectively, inwardly, and personally by the Spirit of God. God takes His Word, and, by His Spirit, He then leads us. John 10:27 is one of my favorite verses, as it drives home this truth in a direct and powerful way:

> *"My sheep hear my voice, and I know them, and they follow me."*

We can hear the voice of our Shepherd when we pray, "Savior, like a shepherd lead us." And the Spirit of God, taking the Word of God, will speak specifically and strategically to us. I don't know how to explain this, I don't know how to define this, and I don't know how to describe this. But I can tell you…having experienced the Spirit's leading in my life… when we surrender to Him in prayer and when we seek Him in His Word…He will lead us by His Spirit.

God will open a door…God will close a door…God will speak through a friend…God's Spirit will speak through a message…God's Spirit will speak internally in our hearts. But God will speak! So be willing to listen to Him when you pray, when you take time to get alone and open up to Him and listen to Him.

So if you are going to pursue the will of God, you must surrender to the will of God, abide in the Word of God, and yield to the Spirit of God.

PRACTICE THE WILL OF GOD

If your desire is to have the will of God done on earth as it is in heaven, then you must not only pray for the will of God and pursue the will of God, but you must practice the will of God.

When Jesus taught us to pray, this is what He said in Matthew 6:10:

> *"Your will be done on earth as it is in heaven" (NKJV).*

The slogan that comes to mind is "Just Do It!" We are to put the will of God into practice!

I believe many Christians come to God and say, "Lord, show me Your will...but I'll decide whether or not I'm going to do it." What

God wants is a heart that is totally yielded and ready and willing to follow Him. A heart that cries out, "Lord, Your will…anytime, anywhere, at any cost!"

As a young preacher, I heard the great preacher Steven Olford say something I have tried to live throughout my life:

> *"God is not responsible to lead us one step further than the measure of our obedience to Him."*

God's not going to show you more of His will if there are already things in your life you know aren't in His will. Why should God lead you forward if there's disobedience in your life? You must be willing to not only *discover* the will of God, but to *do* the will of God on earth as it is in heaven.

Now, I got to thinking about that and began to wonder, how is the will of God done in heaven? Well, it's done passionately, it's done perfectly, and it's done perpetually.

Think about angels, for example. Angels are actively, obediently, and cheerfully doing the will of God at this very moment in heaven. The Bible tells us that in heaven, His servants serve Him day and night. And they never go on strike, never sleep in late, and don't take a long lunch or an extra coffee break! They serve Him actively, aggressively, energetically, and perfectly day and night. There's no sloughing off in heaven. The will of God is done passionately, perfectly, and perpetually.

> IF THE WILL OF GOD IS GOING TO BE DONE IN MY LIFE ON EARTH AS IT IS IN HEAVEN, THEN I NEED TO BE PRAYING IN OBEDIENCE TO HIM THAT I WILL DO THE WILL OF GOD PASSIONATELY, PERFECTLY, AND PERPETUALLY.

And if the will of God is going to be done in my life on earth as it is in heaven, then I need to be praying in obedience to Him that I will do the will of God passionately, perfectly, and perpetually.

The last thing most Christians need today is just another Bible study where we sit still and gather more information...only to do nothing about it. Some people think that the extent of the Christian life is to go to church, endure a sermon, and go home. God hasn't saved us so that we can sit on a pew and listen to somebody talk. Instead, we are saved to serve Him...not to sit, soak, and sour on the bench. By the way, have you ever noticed how bench players can get negative and critical about the people who are playing?

Don't be a bench player. Get in the game and practice the will of God. And if you're going to do the will of God, do it cheerfully and gratefully with all your heart.

Let me add one other word here about how you select a church, because it directly relates to doing and practicing the will of God. So many people today are looking for churches to bless them. While it's fine to seek a church that's going to meet your needs and the needs of your family, let me challenge you instead to look for a place where you can be a blessing, and help to meet other people's needs. That's one of the ways you practice God's will in your life.

God has called us to do His will *now*. And someday, when we get to heaven and stand before Jesus Christ, all of our excuses for not serving Him…for not doing His will…for not being active in the ministry and serving Him…are going to be so lame. Sure we're busy. Yes, we have a job. And of course there are family responsibilities. While all these things are important, we often use them as excuses because we're unwilling to do the will of God with our lives.

Life is doing the will of God. Life is not about how long you live, but how well you live. It's not the duration of your life that really matters, it's the *donation* of your life that counts…what you give, what you contribute…in doing the will of God.

Everything in light of eternity will fade into history. So today, make doing and practicing the will of God your priority. Pray for the will of God. Pursue the will of God. Practice the will of God.

Make your prayer, "Your will be done on earth as it is in heaven."

CHAPTER
THREE
KNOCK

In the last two chapters, we have been looking at the model of prayer Jesus gives us in Matthew 7:

> *"Ask, and it will be given to you; seek, and you will find; knock, and it will be opened to you."*

We've learned that to A-S-K is to ask, seek, and knock. And that means when we call upon God, we unleash the power of prayer as He opens the doors of heaven and pours blessings on us that will amaze us.

Isn't it incredible that the God of heaven, the great God of glory, would have interest in our needs? But He does. He has an infinite interest in each one of us…including you.

And He wants us to keep on asking…to keep on seeking…and to keep on knocking. But what does it mean to "keep on knocking"? If you recall, earlier we learned that:

- Asking is petitioning prayer.
- Seeking is perceiving prayer.
- Knocking is persistent prayer.

So you must keep on knocking…you must be persistent in prayer…if you are to unleash the power of prayer.

Now, most Christians struggle with persistent prayer. And perhaps you do, too. So let me point you to some Scripture that I believe will help you become persistent in prayer.

One of the passages we have looked at as we learn how to pray—and to unleash the power of prayer—is the Lord's Prayer (Matthew 6). This is the model prayer in which Jesus shows us how we are to pray. If you remember, this prayer begins with:

"Our Father in heaven, hallowed be Your name. Your kingdom come. Your will be done on earth as it is in heaven" (NKJV).

If you notice, Jesus begins the prayer by looking to heaven. But the model of prayer takes a turn in verse 11 when Jesus moves us from heaven to the earth…from a focus on seeking God's will to our personal needs and how we can find God's provision and blessing for our lives.

Jesus says in verses 11-13:

"Give us this day our daily bread. And forgive us our debts, as we forgive our debtors. And do not lead us into temptation, but deliver us from the evil one. For Yours is the kingdom and the power and the glory

"GIVE US THIS DAY

OUR DAILY BREAD. AND

FORGIVE US OUR DEBTS, AS WE

FORGIVE OUR DEBTORS. AND

DO NOT LEAD US INTO

TEMPTATION, BUT DELIVER US

FROM THE EVIL ONE."

forever. Amen" (NKJV).

In these three verses, Jesus outlines three reasons why we should be persistent in prayer: *give us*, that is to pray for provision; *forgive us*, that is to pray for pardon; and *deliver us*, that is to pray for protection.

If we are to unleash the power of prayer in our lives, we must make these three things a persistent part of our prayer life. We must "keep on knocking." Let me show you why.

PERSISTENT PRAYER FOR PROVISION

The first thing Jesus instructs us to do is pray for provision. Now, it may not seem all that spiritual to pray, "Lord, give us this day our daily bread" when there's so much "bread" around us. But you need to understand that God is interested in your physical needs just as He is interested in your spiritual needs.

This is a very simple and yet very profound teaching. Our Lord wants us to know that we need to call upon Him for even the most basic necessities of life….for everything we need. He wants us to humbly recognize that even the bread on our table is a gift from Him. He wants us to realize that no matter how much we may earn, no matter how hard we may work, and no matter how cleverly we may invest and save and buy, it is all a gift from Him. Even the abilities to work and the smarts to invest are gifts from God!

Now, you might be thinking, "Why should I pray for daily bread when I have so much?" It's a good question. If we have more than the world has all around us, then why pray for more bread? There are a number of reasons.

First, the fact that we have so much…the

fact that we have more than the rest of the world…actually means we ought to pray now more than ever each day for bread. To do anything other than that is to live in pride, and to live in pride is not to live in dependence upon God. We must recognize that every breath we take and every bite we eat is a gift from God.

When we pray, "Give us this day our daily bread," it expresses our dependence upon God. It expresses our gratitude to God for His daily provision. And how ungrateful we would be if we did not express our thankfulness to God each day for our bread! We must persistently express our dependence on God and our thankfulness to Him for His daily provision.

> WHEN WE PRAY, "GIVE US THIS DAY OUR DAILY BREAD," IT EXPRESSES OUR DEPENDENCE UPON GOD.

Second, this verse also points to our need to live every day one day at a time. When God delivered manna, or bread, to the children of Israel, He did so day by day. It was bread for the day, and they were to use it up that day. And if they tried to store it up, it spoiled. God gave them just enough bread for every day. And that is the way God wants us to live. He wants us to come to Him every day, asking Him for daily bread and the miracle of His blessings. And as we are persistent in this prayer, we demonstrate our dependence on living from His hand to our mouth.

HE WANTS US TO COME TO HIM EVERY DAY, ASKING HIM FOR DAILY BREAD AND THE MIRACLE OF HIS BLESSINGS.

Did you know that Jesus is committed to meeting your personal needs, your physical needs, and, yes, your material needs? Let me give you a few Scripture verses that you may want to underline in your Bible. The first is Romans 8:32, where Paul says:

> *He who did not spare his own Son but gave him up for us all, how will he not also with him graciously give us all things?*

God delights to give to us. When we are persistent in prayer for our daily provision, God is delighted to provide for us! It's been said, "Prayer is not overcoming God's reluctance, but it is laying hold of His highest willingness to bless us."

Our Father doesn't come to us with closed or clenched fists, but with an open hand and an open heart. He hears the cries of His children. He is the Father who has given us His Son! And don't you think if He has given us His Son, He will also give us everything we need?

AND MY GOD WILL

SUPPLY EVERY NEED OF YOURS

ACCORDING TO HIS RICHES IN

GLORY IN CHRIST JESUS.

The second verse I want to give you is Philippians 4:19, which is a familiar passage. This powerful verse tells us:

And my God will supply every need of yours according to his riches in glory in Christ Jesus.

Take a moment to meditate on that verse. What the Scripture is telling us is that all we need and more is multiplied in our lives when we call upon Him. There is no need too great. Is there a need in your life today? If you will turn to God, He will supply that need. Now, He may not do it as you think He should or when you think He should, but He will supply it…in His wisdom and according to His riches! God wants to provide for your every need.

The next verse I want to give you is found in 2 Corinthians 9:10-11:

He who supplies seed to the sower and bread for food will supply and multiply your seed for sowing and increase the harvest of your righteousness. You will be enriched in every way for all your generosity, which through us will produce thanksgiving to God.

GOD HAS BLESSED US ABUNDANTLY SO THAT WE ARE ABLE TO GIVE TO OTHERS.

Do you see what Paul is saying? We're overcome with the blessings of God! He has blessed us abundantly, and why? God has blessed us abundantly so that we are able to give to others. If you've been given more than enough bread, then God has called upon you to share your bread and share your possessions with others. So be thankful for the abundance God has provided in your life…and be ready to share it!

The next verse that shows God's desire to provide for us is one of my favorite verses of Scripture. It is Psalm 37:25. It's especially powerful when you realize just how much David understood his need to depend upon the Lord for daily bread and daily needs:

I have been young, and now am old,
yet I have not seen the righteous forsaken
or his children begging for bread.

Why? Because God supplies our needs, when we call upon Him…when we keep on knocking.

The last verse I want to give you is 1 Chronicles 29:14. This verse is part of a larger passage in which David is coming to the end of His life and the nation of Israel has gathered to give a generous offering to build the temple…something that has been a passion for all of David's years as king of Israel. So in response to such a generous offering, David prays to God:

> *"But who am I, and what is my people, that we should be able thus to offer willingly? For all things come from you, and of your own have we given you."*

Anything we are able to give is what we have been given by God. He has blessed us, and because of that blessing, we should look to give generously. What we are to do with the bread that we have been given as we depend upon God every day is to eat what we need and to use what we need, but then to share generously and bountifully with others.

WHEN WE PRAY FOR GOD'S PROVISION EVERY DAY, IT MEANS THAT WE TRUST HIM.

When we pray for God's provision every day, it means that we trust Him.

And as Jesus explains later on in the book of Matthew, if God takes care of birds, He will take care of you. And if He clothes the lilies of the field, He will clothe you. You are not to worry. Instead of worrying, pray. Pray persistently…keep on knocking for your daily bread…and you will experience the joy of life in receiving from the hand of God these great blessings of life.

That is the importance of persistent prayer for provision.

PERSISTENT PRAYER FOR PARDON

In verse 12 of Matthew 6, Jesus tells us:

"And forgive us our debts, as we forgive our debtors" (NKJV).

Every person…yes, every Christian…needs forgiveness because we all have sinned. Now, sin is described in numerous ways in the Bible. For example, sin is described as a disease. It is a disease that produces spiritual death. The Bible also describes sin as disobedience to God. Sin is also described as darkness—spiritual darkness—and as a defilement.

It's no wonder that the psalmist David cried out, "Wash me thoroughly…"!

The way in which the Bible describes sin seems almost endless. Sin is portrayed as defiance, trespassing against God, transgressing, rebellion against the will of God, and as a defect. The very word *sin* means missing the mark or falling short…that we are incomplete and defective in our human personalities. Sin is also described as a distortion. The word is "iniquity," which means perverseness or crookedness… "bent" in the Hebrew. Sin perverts God's original intention. God gives us a desire, and when we abuse and pervert that desire, it becomes sin.

Sin is also described in the Bible as deceit or a deception. That's why it's so hard for people to admit their sin or to admit the severity of their sin. Many will admit their sin but they don't see the big deal. But with God, sin is huge. And it is a mistake of the highest proportion to spend our days hiding, lying, and covering our sin.

> IF WE ARE TO UNLEASH THE POWER OF PRAYER IN OUR LIVES, WE NEED TO COME CLEAN WITH GOD ON A DAILY BASIS, TO KEEP SHORT ACCOUNTS WITH GOD.

If we are to unleash the power of prayer in our lives, we need to come clean with God on a daily basis, to keep short accounts with God. Because David tells us in Psalm 66:18:

> *If I had cherished iniquity in my heart,*
> *the Lord would not have listened.*

While there are many promises in Scripture that God will answer prayer…that when we call on God, He hears us and will answer us…this verse makes it clear that God promises *not* to answer our prayers if we cherish iniquity in our heart.

What does it mean to "cherish iniquity" in your heart? It means that you are holding on to sin…you are keeping sin as a pet. If you cherish sin and live in sin rather than confessing your sin and coming clean with God, then God says He's just going to hold you off and not hear you. Some people don't think they need forgiveness, but that's a lie. As someone once said, "The greater the saint, the greater the sense of sin and the need for forgiveness." When you dare to draw near into the presence of the Holy God, you realize and recognize your own sinfulness.

So sin is described in various ways, but

"...FORGIVE US OUR

DEBTS, AS WE FORGIVE

OUR DEBTORS."

when Jesus chose to describe sin and our need for forgiveness, He said that sin is like a debt.

"...forgive us our debts, as we forgive our debtors"(NKJV).

Now, if you're in financial debt, one thing you can do is go to a financial counselor. And the first thing that financial counselor is going to do is to help you measure the full extent of your indebtedness. You have to know how much you owe before you can begin to pay it back.

WE ARE IN GOD'S ETERNAL DEBT BECAUSE WE HAVE BEEN FORGIVEN, FULLY AND FREELY.

When we come to God, we need to realize our debt and recognize our indebtedness to Him. We need to ask, "How much do I owe God?" Well, we owe Him our very lives. Every breath we take comes from Him. Our lives are on loan from Him. He made

us, and He keeps us alive…and that is a debt
that we owe. We also owe Him obedience. And
as followers of Jesus, we owe Him our best. We
are to glorify Him.

But when we talk about the debt we owe
God, there is the debt of sin—and there is hell to
pay for our sin and our rebellion. It is a debt so
insurmountable that not one of us can dig out of
the bankruptcy of this debt. So God, in His love
and His grace, gave us the forgiveness of sin.
And He made this forgiveness possible by the
blood of Jesus, His Son, who died on the cross
to pay our sin debt…to forgive us of our sins,
past, present, and future. We are in God's
eternal debt because we have been forgiven,
fully and freely.

This truth is illustrated so powerfully and so
beautifully in the story of the prodigal son.
When that son, who rebelled against his father

and was broken by his sin and rebellion, came home, his father ran to him and welcomed him home...he embraced him...even as God our Father welcomes us home when we come back to Him.

In Colossians 2:14, the apostle Paul tells us that Jesus took the debt that was against us, what we owed, and He nailed it to the cross. No wonder Philip Bliss wrote in his hymn "It Is Well With My Soul":

> *My sin, not in part but the whole,*
> *Is nailed to the cross, and I bear it no more,*
> *Praise the Lord, praise the Lord, O my soul!*

We have been forgiven, and as children of God, we can come to Him persistently and continually, bringing the sin that He forgives. And when we turn from our sin and trust in Him and His forgiveness, we not only have eternal life, we experience abundant life. Rather than living in the defeat and debt and under the weight of sin, we're set free from its bondage.

And any person who is in bondage to sin can be forgiven…and changed and cleansed from within. Don't believe the lies of our culture and society…which have given in to Satan himself…that suggest that some are born to a manner of life and they cannot change. No matter who you are and what you have done, you can be set free from the debt and bondage of sin in Jesus Christ.

> NO MATTER WHO YOU ARE AND WHAT YOU HAVE DONE, YOU CAN BE SET FREE FROM THE DEBT AND BONDAGE OF SIN IN JESUS CHRIST.

One final word on this passage, which says:

"…forgive us our debts, as we forgive our debtors"(NKJV).

Jesus' grace and forgiveness are available

to all who call upon Him. He is not putting a condition on salvation, but rather giving a characteristic of a person who knows Jesus and has been forgiven. To put it simply, those who have been forgiven will forgive, and being a forgiver is essential to your well-being as a believer and as a person.

YOU'RE NEVER MORE LIKE JESUS THAN WHEN YOU'RE EXTENDING THE FORGIVENESS AND THE LOVE AND THE GRACE THAT HE HAS GIVEN YOU.

To harbor resentment or anger or hatred will bring your spiritual life and your prayer life to a standstill. You will never unleash the power of prayer in your life if you are not forgiving. When I'm helping young couples prepare for marriage, I tell them that every marriage needs two things...two good givers and two good forgivers. Because in every relationship there will be hurts, insults, problems, and difficulties. And the only way to survive…and thrive…in a relationship is to forgive.

That's why Jesus tells us to forgive as we have been forgiven. He knows we're going to be hurt and hurt one another intentionally or unintentionally. So be someone who is ready to extend forgiveness. Don't follow the lead of our culture which exalts vengeance…getting even. Instead, forgive, even as Christ has forgiven you. You're never more like Jesus than when you're extending the forgiveness and the love and the grace that He has given you.

PERSISTENT PRAYER FOR PROTECTION

The final verse in this passage says:

"And do not lead us into temptation, but deliver us from the evil one"(NKJV).

Jesus wants us to pray persistently…to

"keep on knocking"...for protection and deliverance from Satan. And if you are to unleash the power of prayer in your life, this is an essential truth you must practice!

You need to understand that Satan is a powerful enemy. Because you are a believer and a follower of Jesus Christ, he is determined to sabotage your every effort for God...to subvert the witness of Christ in your life. And, my friend, every day is a battle.

Paul writes in Ephesians 6:11-12:

> *Put on the whole armor of God, that you may be able to stand against the schemes of the devil. For we do not wrestle against flesh and blood, but against the rulers, against the authorities, against the cosmic powers over this present darkness, against the spiritual forces of evil in the heavenly places.*

The devil's attacks in your life are premeditated and very real. If you're a follower of Christ, temptation is a reality, and Satan is actively doing all he can to keep you from following Christ. If you feel like you have never met the devil, it's probably because you're going in the same direction he's going! If you turn around and live

> AND WHEN WE PRAY FOR PROTECTION, GOD DELIVERS US.

for Christ, you'll meet him face to face.

But you need not fear his assault. In fact, every temptation…every time we engage in spiritual battle with the enemy of our soul…is an opportunity for us to grow stronger in our faith. When we recognize our frailties, our vulnerabilities, our temptations, and our weaknesses, we will pray for spiritual power to defeat the enemy. And when we pray for protection, God delivers us.

You'll never outgrow temptation. But remember, it's not a sin to be tempted. Don't beat yourself up because you're still tempted and you're still dealing with some of the same vulnerabilities and sinful propensities that you've had from your past. Those temptations are a prime reason why you need to keep on asking, keep on seeking, and keep on knocking. You need to be persistent in your prayers that the Lord will protect you and deliver you.

> WHEN WE PRAY PERSISTENTLY FOR PROTECTION, WE ARE HUMBLY RECOGNIZING OUR WEAKNESSES AND VULNERABILITIES… AND ASKING GOD TO DELIVER US FROM THEM.

In one sense, you should consider the fact that you're tempted a privilege, because Satan considers you worth attacking. He sees you as a target…there's a contract out on you, if you will. So it's vitally important that you know what your weaknesses are and that you don't give the devil an opportunity or an opening to tempt you. That's why it's vital for you to pray that God would protect you, that He would guard and guide your steps and deliver you from evil.

In his New Testament commentary, John MacArthur says the following about this passage:

> *This prayer is an appeal to God to place a watch over our eyes, our ears, our mouths, our feet and our hands that in whatever we see, hear or say and in any place we go and in anything we do, He will protect us from sin.*

When we pray persistently for protection, we are humbly recognizing our weaknesses and vulnerabilities...and asking God to deliver us from them. But when we fail to pray persistently, we are allowing pride and arrogance to direct us. That's why 1 Corinthians 10:12 tells us, "…let anyone who thinks that he stands take heed lest he fall."

I tell you, in my own life I run just a little bit scared, because I have a worthy respect for my adversary, and I know my own vulnerabilities and weaknesses. I know it's essential that I get on my knees…that I get in the presence of God…and say, "Lord, protect me this day, watch over me." We all need to ask God for His protection and deliverance. And we all need to recognize that God will give us power to defeat our temptations.

Why are we constantly getting knocked down? I think it's because we fail to pray first thing in the morning. We need to pray in advance of our temptations.

So often we get beaten, bruised, knocked

down, and whipped every day…and then we fall on our knees at our bedsides and say, "Lord, I did it again, please forgive me of all my sins." And while our God is a God of grace and will forgive us, wouldn't it be much better if God would protect us, and in that temptation provide an exit strategy for us? Remember, God will never put any more on us than He will put in us to overcome every obstacle of faith. But we need to persistently pray for that deliverance.

> REMEMBER, GOD WILL NEVER PUT ANY MORE ON US THAN HE WILL PUT IN US TO OVERCOME EVERY OBSTACLE OF FAITH.

So again, we ought to run just a little bit scared, knowing that the evil one is "like a roaring lion, seeking someone to devour"…and that temptation is all around us.

I heard about a Christian college several

years ago that said you should send your kids there because it was 17 miles from any known sin. But there's no place that's safe, because the enemy is at work within us and temptations assail us. But God will deliver us...if we pray for that deliverance.

In that great hymn "A Mighty Fortress Is Our God," Martin Luther wrote:

And though this world, with devils filled, should threaten to undo us, We will not fear, for God hath willed His truth to triumph through us: The Prince of Darkness grim, we tremble not for him; His rage we can endure, for lo, his doom is sure, One little word shall fell him.

And what is that word? It is the Word of Christ. It's like the little girl who said, "When I hear Satan knocking at the door I just say, 'Jesus would you mind getting that?'"

PUT ON THE WHOLE

ARMOR OF GOD, THAT YOU MAY

BE ABLE TO STAND AGAINST THE

SCHEMES OF THE DEVIL.

If we pray for protection, God will deliver us. When Satan seeks to destroy us, when Satan attacks the people of God, His Church, know this: The gates of hell will not prevail against it. And one great day...one glorious day...we will be delivered from sin and the attacks of the enemy, and we will leave the field of battle and march home in victory to receive the victor's crown and forever be in the presence of Jesus. That is our confidence in Christ!

SO KEEP ON KNOCKING... PRAYING PERSISTENTLY FOR PROVISION, PARDON, AND PROTECTION.

But as we battle here on earth, and we stumble and fall, God will forgive us of our sins. He's promised that. But isn't it better to be delivered of sins? Isn't it better to pray that God would deliver us from sin and the slavery of sin? So persistently pray for God's protection. And as you do, you will unleash the power of prayer in your life.

I look back on my life as a young teenager…and throughout my days as a Christian…and I see how God answered my prayers and protected me from evil and gave me grace in the midst of temptations. And I know that it was not my own power, but the power of Jesus in answering prayer.

So keep on knocking…praying persistently for provision, pardon, and protection.

A FINAL WORD

Jesus, when He closes this great model prayer, does so with a doxology. Because in praising God in prayer, we recognize the source of all power and unleash the power of prayer.

> *"For Yours is the kingdom and the*
> *power and the glory forever. Amen"*
> *(NKJV).*

This closing doxology by Jesus is an echo of the Old Testament prayer of David in 1 Chronicles 29. It's a recognition of the greatness and glory...and POWER...that is God's and God's alone. And it is that power that is unleashed when we pray the way Jesus instructed us to pray.

It is a prayer that begins with the Father who hears us and sees us in secret, and closes with a King who, in sympathy, hears us in His sovereignty and delivers us from the power and attack of the evil one.

> *"Ask, and it will be given to you; seek, and you will find; knock, and it will be opened to you."*

So commit today to keep on asking…keep on seeking…and keep on knocking!

Please call 1-800-779-7693 or visit powerpoint.org/resources to order the following products:

Revealing the Fraud of the Da Vinci Code	$ 6.95
Triumph! How You Can Overcome Death and Gain Eternal Life	$ 7.95
The Truth About Influence	$ 6.95
Experiencing God's Peace in a Pressure Cooker World	$ 2.95
Is the Bible Just Another Book?	$ 2.95
Dealing with Doubt	$ 2.95
Rock Solid	$ 2.95
Marriage by the Book	$ 2.95
How to Raise Sexually Pure Kids	$ 2.95
Kingdom First	$ 2.95
True Womanhood	$ 2.95
New Life in Christ	$ 2.95
Stress Test	$ 2.95

These and other booklets by Jack Graham are available at quantity discounts.

Life according to Jesus	$12.99
Diamonds in the Dark	$16.99
A Hope and a Future	$12.99
Lessons from the Heart	$18.95
A Man of God	$17.99

1-800-414-7693 (1-800-414-POWER)
jgraham@powerpoint.org
jackgraham.org